TO THE
WORLD'S
GREATEST
DAD!

The C.R. Gibson Company
Norwalk, Connecticut.

Dad — Thanks for being you.

IN PRAISE OF FATHER

FATHER. . .what images this one word brings to mind! Strong shoulders for watching a parade from, a secure hand to guide you on your first shaky bike ride, someone to look up to — not only because when we're children fathers are much taller, but more importantly, because a child feels that a father is someone to love and admire.

FATHER. . .who can be called upon to mend a broken toy (or heart). . .who knows the answers to questions like: "What holds an airplane up?" or — later, much later — "Shall I marry him, Dad?"

FATHER. . .who advances a loan on your allowance when you're little, and lets you borrow the car when you're just old enough to drive.

FATHER. . .a guide when you're uncertain, a pal when you need companionship, a teacher when you want to widen your horizons, a confidant when you've got a problem, a friend when others fail you.

FATHER. . .someone who's always proud of your smallest accomplishments, who always encourages your ideas, who helps you build your dreams, who loves you no matter what, who would do anything in the world for you to make you happy!

Katherine Nelson Davis

WHAT IS A FATHER?

A father should be the first one the child would think of communicating with when overwhelmed by physical woes, emotional problems, confusing philosophies, conflicting ideas about what he is to do. A father is meant to be a shelter. A shelter shuts out wind, rain, ice, cold, heat, sand, mosquitos, or armies of men. A father is meant to be a strong tower of protection. The very word "father" should conjure up a feeling of security.

Edith Schaeffer

FATHER KNEW ALL THE ANSWERS

I cannot remember ever failing to get an answer from Father, no matter how advanced or complex my question. It now has dawned on me that Father's theory was that you could not deny a child an answer, *some* answer, *any* answer. I would ask, "What happened to dinosaurs?" and he would answer without a second's hesitation, "The saber-toothed tigers ate 'em up."

"What happened to the saber-toothed tigers?"
"They froze in the Ice Age."
"When was the Ice Age?"
"Thousands of years ago."
"Before Christ?"
"Yep. Ten million years before Christ, to be exact."

Kindly and brilliant soul that he was, Father could not bear to let us down. We asked, he answered. He also answered any and all questions thrown at him by the neighborhood kids, their parents, the grocer, traveling salesmen, farmers, and professors of Egyptology from the university. There is no instance in recorded or remembered history when Father ever said, "I don't know."

Jonathan Rhoades

Quiet, loving moments shared by a father and his baby son. . .

Spring days that I didn't teach or have seminars, I walked with Thomas. I would perch him in the back carrier and hike. You couldn't see the baby up there behind you but you could feel him warm against your back, riding, and soon falling asleep, bumping gently against you with each step.

We lived on the edge of old woods and I walked for hours some afternoons through the pines and scrub down to a long thin lake that in winter had deer tracks across it in the snow like punctuation. I remember sitting on a rock in the sun one hot blue spring day, watching a striped grey snake work off his skin against a fallen pine. Thomas slept the whole time and I have never felt quieter in my life.

Robert Miner

FROM FATHER TO SON: PLEASURE

Every father is special in a different way. Leo Rosten paints a moving word portrait of his Papa.

My mother and father were immensely proud, and he somewhat in awe, of my scholastic efforts. I learned as a boy that I could usually get out of a chore — taking out the garbage, sifting the ashes in the cellar for unburned coal, pasting labels on the sweater boxes in the store (our living room) — by picking up a book. And when my father saw me reading, he would pat me on the head, saying, "That's good, that's good; you're laying in stock — " tapping his temple — "up here!" He never ceased to marvel over the miracles that came from men's minds.

I never knew a man who so loved newspapers. He read them with the utmost care, savoring every item. He could derive pleasure from every story — whether world-shaking or picayune. He even devoured the space fillers. He would pore through his bifocals over the speech of a President or the yarn of a two-headed calf, marveling and clucking and tchk-tchking: "Imagine!" "How do you like that?" "Who could expect such a thing?"

He particularly enjoyed interviews; he read any interview with anyone — a scientist, an actress, a lifeguard, a thief. To him, the morning paper renewed the newness of life each day, without fail: a glorious bazaar, a circus of wonders and follies, a forum, a sideshow, a school, a stage.

He loved to make people laugh. He could not wait to tell you the latest joke or story he had heard; and no one enjoyed hearing a story more.

He had an instinct for the amusing aspect of any event, even the most commonplace, and he often tricked us into laughter with delicious nonsense. He would exclaim with excitement,

"*Guess* who I met this morning?"

"Who?"

"The mailman."

Or he would slap his knee as if he had just thought of something frightfully important: "How could I forget to tell you? *Guess* what I found, right on the street?"

"What?"

"A handkerchief."

Do these stories sound absurd? You have no idea what delight they gave me, for it flattered me to see my father trying to please me; and it impressed me to think a man could find such an amplitude of pleasure in pleasing a child.

CRAYONS

You ask me how God felt on that first day.
I think I know:
With paper and a new box of bright crayons
I have felt just so —
The children pressing at each elbow
("Draw a sunset and a polar bear!")
. . . But even God was not so lucky —
He had no audience there.

Christopher Morley

FOR FATHER'S DAY

Here a little child I wait
Father dear, beside our gate.
When the sun is dropping low
And tired birds to branches go
That's the time I would not roam
Lest I miss your coming home.
And if God should chance to be
Looking from the sky at me
He would smile there in the blue
For He is Our Father, too.

Rachel Field

THE THINGS MY CHILDREN TAUGHT ME

One of the best things about children is their
humanizing influence. You have to deal with them
on their level. You cannot impress them with your
title or your prestige or your bluster. You cannot
hide from them. You have to relate to them directly
as people, and that is something many of us don't
do very often. Talk about reducing life to
simplicities! Trying to communicate with a child is
one of the simplest acts imaginable. Just the two of
you. When it's not driving you crazy ("Why?"
"Because. . .") it can be wonderfully refreshing.

Children also force you to re-evaluate your
priorities. They keep you honest. When Lee was old
enough to realize when I was away from home, the
first long trip I took was to Alaska. I brought back
some high rubber boots, and occasionally he will
drag them out of the closet and put them on.
Sometimes the boots will remind him of the trip,
and he will say something like, "I miss you very

much when you go away." You have to confront that; you have to decide what is more important, he or another trip somewhere.

Most of all, children teach the capacity for enjoyment. The ecstasy a child can find in a carrot or an apple is simply amazing. They like to run just for the fun of it, or stick their heads out the window of the car to feel the wind. They can break through all those levels of control, all those accretions of detachment and sobriety that plug up your laugh ducts. When I come home at night and the two of them burst through the door, running down the walk to greet me, the world is a beautiful place. No matter what else has happened, it's beautiful.

When you are really in love, you think you are the first person who has ever felt that way. Parenthood should be the same way. I don't care if it's trite—I love to hear my children laugh, just as I love to see my wife standing in the doorway, watching us.

Steven V. Roberts

A DAUGHTER'S SMILE

What would an ideal daughter be like from a father's point of view? She would be a normal, sane, self-reliant young woman who is just beginning to discover that she is a person and a personality, with all the faults and all the virtues which that implies. She is one who realizes that she doesn't surrender her individuality by consulting and being guided by her Father and her Mother, and one who makes it part of her daily living to share with them her companionship, friendship and affection.

And, parents, if you want to learn what the ideal daughter is like, it is quite simple. You have only to look up now and then from your preoccupation and you will see her, sitting in the big chair across the room from you, all curled up like a kitten with her feet on the furniture, ready to smile back at you in answer to your smile.

Josef J. Hayes

From the confessions of a full-time mothering father of a two-year-old whirlwind.

I love the surprises my daughter offers me, her quickness, her spontaneity. I love her curiosity, even when it embarrasses me — like the other day in the public library.

We had gone to the library, Gillian and I, so I could check out some books on — what else — child care. After a prolonged detour at the card catalogues which had to be opened, riffled through, shut, hidden behind and crawled under, we finally made it to the section where the books on child care are kept.

I spotted a book that looked interesting and plucked it off the shelf, while Gillian, for once, stood quietly beside me. Ah yes, little one, I thought, you are all tuckered out from pillaging the card catalogue. So I relaxed and started skimming through the book. Gillian squatted down and looked at the books on the bottom shelf, her hand harmlessly brushing along the spines. All's well, I thought, and then I became engrossed in a passage. Suddenly I heard a clatter. Next, footsteps running. I looked down for my daughter. She had, of course, disappeared. Then I heard a tiny voice call, "Cir-cul! Circul!"

I raced down the aisle and around the corner of the stacks. There was Gillian, seated, surrounded by at least twenty fat books, one huge tome spread open on her lap. She was looking up into the eyes of a man, who towered over her, hands on hips.

She pointed to the page, saying earnestly to him, "Cir-cul! Circul!"

The man turned to me, "Is this your child?" he asked, his voice expressionless.

"Yes, I think so," I replied, bending down for a closer look.

The man looked at me and shook his head. I had visions of the two of us being banished from the library, like Adam and Eve, forever.

Then the man smiled. He chuckled. He reached down and patted her head. "She's about two, isn't she?"

"Yes."

"Nothing like a two-year-old," he said, wagging his head from side to side sagely. "Had a couple myself."

I gathered Gillian up into my arms, and we went to the desk, where we checked out two books on the psychology and development of children.

Clutching the books and carrying my first-born on my shoulders, I waited for the traffic light to change. Suddenly Gillian shouted, "Daddy. You're my Daddy!" as if she were making a discovery. And she bent down and planted a hearty kiss on my cheek. And another on the other cheek. And I was glad that my efforts to tame and subdue a bit of Gillian's irrepressible style had not yet met with much success.

Jack McGarvey

TRANSPORTATION PROBLEM

Kiddy cars of little tikes,
Slightly older children's bikes,
Skis and sleds for winter needs,
Wagons, trucks, velocipedes,
Skooters, ice (and roller) skates —
How the stuff accumulates —
Piles of articles vehicular,
On the front porch in particular,
Things your children go like heck on,
And you fall and break your neck on.

Richard Armour

Happy is the father behind the wheels of his own baby's carriage.

A father pushing a baby carriage is supposed to be the very symbol of a henpecked husband.

Actually, though, taking the baby for a solo stroll is one of the great pleasures of fatherhood. It's so pleasant, in fact, that the politic husband may deem it wise to conceal his enjoyment.

"All right, all *right*," he should snap irritably when his wife suggests that he take the baby out for some air. "If you want all the neighbors to laugh up their sleeves at me, then all *right*."

The deliberate, measured pacing, with occasional pauses to maneuver the carriage up and down curbstones, gives him a splendid opportunity to show off his offspring. The motion of the carriage causes the baby to smile beatifically. And Poppa himself feels a heady flush of self-importance, because the baby's been entrusted to his care.

As a conversation piece, nothing — not even a brace of French poodles wearing crocheted hug-me-tights — holds a candle to a grinning baby lying flat on its back in a carriage, with its cunning, chubby legs poked rakishly into the air.

It is a heartening sight to watch two carriage-pushing fathers meet on the sidewalk or in a park. Although they may be complete strangers, they have a warm smile for each other and, in a matter of moments, will probably be comparing formulas, weights, teeth, and diaper rash. The spirit of camaraderie which emerges, as they discuss diphtheria shots and how to sleep through noisy tantrums, renews one's faith in the brotherhood of man. Certainly we are not all going to rub out each other in some sort of global pique, so long as two strangers who meet in a park are cuffing each other on the back and punching each other on the upper arm muscle before you can say boo-daddy. And regardless of race, creed, color, and Republicans and Democrats, too.

Frank Gilbreth, Jr.

ANOTHER PROUD DAD SPEAKS. . .

I'm now a full-fledged member of the great community of parents. When my fellow members launch into long spiels about their kids, I listen with patience, confident that they're honor-bound to play fair and let me have my turn — no vulgar bragging, of course.

My sons are now grown and, of course, think they know all the answers. They'll learn better as they get older. Look at how much I've learned since I was their age.

You could say that I've grown up with them. I've learned how to tolerate proud parents by becoming one myself, and to love children instead of being frightened by them. Years ago, I would have found it impossible to believe that one day I would cherish parenthood.

John Finn

ONE MORNING

I remember my littlest one in a field
running so hard at the morning in him
he kicked the heads off daisies. Oh, wild
and windy and spilling over the brim
of his sun-up juices he ran
in the dew of himself. My son.

And the white flower heads
shot like sparks where his knees
pumped, and his hot-shod
feet took off from time, as who knows
when ever again a running morning will be
so light-struck, flower-sparked-full between him and me.

John Ciardi

Poetic tributes to fathers by experts, children. . .

DAD

There are many people in the world,
All sizes, big and small;
But of all the people that I know,
My dad is best of all.
He never was a president,
He never stopped a war;
But in our home my father's king,
When he walks in the door.
He'll help me with my homework,
Though it's not always right.
He'll comfort me when I am scared,
Or when I've had a fight.
He's the average working man,
Never got a Ph.D.
He never won a medal,
But he's best for mom and me.

Connie Vanco

MY FATHER

My father is black.
Black and beautiful.
I think I'll call him my own.
He's sweet, kind, generous, patient,
He's mine.
He's slick, sly, I think I'll call him
    the sweetest man alive.
He's cool and doesn't act like a fool,
    and follows all of the rules.
Well, I guess that's all,
Oh yes, that's what I call my dad.
I don't know about you,
But I think this is true
He's the best father by far.

                    Dawn Belt

With Daddy. That's the best way to go anyplace.

WALKING

When Daddy
Walks
With Jean and me,
We have a
Lot of fun
'Cause we can't
Walk as fast
As he,
Unless we
Skip and
Run!
I stretch,
And stretch
My legs so far,
I nearly slip
And fall —
But how
Does Daddy
Take such steps?
He doesn't stretch
At all!

Grace Ellen Glaubitz

COLLECT CALL

"Hello, I have a collect call from Miss Joyce Robinson in Oshkosh, Wisconsin. Will you accept the charges?"

"Yes, operator, we will."

"Hi, Pops. How are you?"

"Fine. What are you doing in Oshkosh? I thought you were driving to Cape Cod to visit Aunt Rose."

"We were, but Cynthia wanted to stop off and visit a boy she knew from school who lives in Minneapolis."

"Who is Cynthia?"

"She's a girl I met in New Orleans."

"New Orleans? I didn't know you went to New Orleans."

"I wasn't planning to, but Tommy said there was a great concert of the Grateful Dead scheduled to play in the stadium. He got the day right, but the wrong month."

"Tommy?"

"He was hitchhiking on Ninety-five."

"You started out with Ellen Mulberry. Where is she?"

"She met some kids she knew in Fort Lauderdale, and they were driving to Mexico, so she decided to go with them."

"Do Mr. and Mrs. Mulberry know this?"

"I think Ellen called them after the accident."

"What accident?"

"The camper she was in had a blowout, and Ellen got banged up a little."

"So you're now traveling with Cynthia and Tommy."

"No. Tommy stayed in New Orleans, and Cynthia left yesterday. She said she couldn't wait until my car was fixed."

"What's wrong with your car?"

"The motor fell out. That's what I'm calling you about. The garageman said it will cost five hundred and fifty dollars to fix it up."

"That's a fortune!"

"You don't have to pay it if you don't want to. I can leave the car here. I met a guy who has a motorcycle, and he says he'll take me as far as Detroit."

"I'LL PAY IT!"

"How's Mom?"

"She's on the extension. I think she was fine until we got your call. Where are you staying until you get your car fixed?"

"I met some nice kids who have a religious commune near here, and they said I could stay with them if I promise to devote the rest of my life to God."

"That's nice."

"The only problem is I have to shave my head."

"Can't you stay at a motel?"

"I don't have any money left."

"What happened to the three hundred dollars I gave you?"

"Two hundred went for expenses, and one hundred of it went for the fine."

"What fine?"

"We were fined one hundred dollars for speeding in this little itty-bitty town in Arkansas."

"I told you not to drive fast."

"I wasn't driving. Fred was."

"Who the hell is Fred?"

"He's a vegetarian, and he says capitalism is finished in the West."

"That's worth one hundred dollars to hear. Are you going to Cape Cod to visit Aunt Rose or aren't you?"

"As soon as I get the car fixed, Pops. Send me the money care of Western Union. You don't want the man to fix the dented door at the same time?"

"Your car had no dented door."

"It does now. I have to go, Dad. Some kids I met are going to take me white-water canoeing. Good-bye. And, Pops – have a nice day."

Art Buchwald

IF YOU CAN YEARN FOR IT. . .
. . .YOU CAN EARN FOR IT.

We had a permissive father. He permitted us to work. Moral support was all Papa would afford to give us.

Papa was impressed by a newspaper story reporting that Rin Tin Tin earned over $200,000 a year. "And *we* had to have children," Papa lamented.

"I'd like to go to college," brother Joe said to Papa, and Papa encouraged him: "Somebody's stopping you?"

Often Papa would prod us with, "You know what Lincoln was doing at your age?" We knew what Lincoln was doing at Papa's age, but we knew better than to bring that up.

I learned from experience that if there was something lacking, it might turn up if I went after it, saved up for it, worked for it, but never if I just waited for it. Of course, you had to be lucky, too, although I discovered that the more I hustled the luckier I seemed to get. Besides, most of the happiness was in the pursuit.

As my Uncle Benny used to say, "It's not the sugar that makes the tea sweet, but the stirring."

Papa helped each of us get started on the road to success: "Remember, my son, if you ever need a helping hand, you'll find one at the end of your arm. And remember, too, if you want your dreams to come true, don't sleep."

Sam Levinson

King George V was noted for his frugality and thrift, qualities he tried to instill in his offspring. The then Prince of Wales, on the other hand, was pretty much of a spendthrift. While at school, he wrote his father pleading for some additional money. In return he received a stiff note of reproval urging him to change his ways and learn to be a businessman. In the next mail the king found a note from his son which said:

"I have taken your advice. Have just sold your letter to a collector for 25 pounds."

Louis Sobol

FATHERHOOD. Today, a more rewarding role than ever!

We are in a time of real transition. We fathers are trying to define ourselves. We know that we want to play active roles in our children's lives but in order to do that, we must do it every day, not just when the children are old enough to amuse us.

It takes time and energy to establish real human relationships.

Now children can look to both parents for continuous emotional support because there's been a history of commitment. In other words, men's human priorities are changing. And even if his own memory is of a working father who was so busy he never had any time or energy left for his children, the modern father is determined to avoid living that way.

Dr. Sol Gordon

Change is in the air. Father is becoming an increasingly involved parent. The phantom figure who brings home the paycheck and disappears behind the newspaper may be a vanishing breed.

Geraldine Carro

SOME OF MY BEST FRIENDS ARE CHILDREN

Ichneumons are fond of little ichneumons,
And lions of little lions,
But I am not fond of little humans;
I do not believe in scions.

Of course there's always our child,
But our child is different,
Our child appeals
To the cultivated mind.
Ours is a lady;
Boys are odoriferant;
Ladies are the sweetness;
Boys are the rind.

Whenever whimsy collides with whimsy
As parents compare their cherubs,
At the slightest excuse, however flimsy,
I fold my tent like the Arabs.

Of course there's always our child,
But our child is charminger,
Our child's eyes
Are a special kind of blue;
Our child's smile
Is quite a lot disarminger;
Our child's tooth
Is very nearly through.

Mankind, I consider, attained its zenith
The day it achieved the adult;
When the conversation to infants leaneth,
My horse is bridled and saddult.

Of course there's always our child,
But our child is wittier;
Our child's noises
Are the nicest kind of noise;
She has no beard
Like Tennyson or Whittier;
But Tennyson and Whittier
Began as little boys.

The Politician, the Parent, the Preacher,
Were each of them once a kiddie.
The child is indeed a talented creature.
O I want one? Oh, God forbidde!

But now there's always our child,
And our child's adorable.
Our child's an angel
Fairer than the flowers;
Our child fascinates
One who's rather borable;
And incidentally,
Our child is ours.

Ogden Nash

A PRAYER FOR FATHER

Mender of toys, leader of boys,
Changer of fuses, kisser of bruises,
Bless him, dear Lord.
Mover of couches, soother of ouches,
Pounder of nails, teller of tales,
Reward him, O Lord.
Hanger of screens, counselor of teens,
Fixer of bikes, chastiser of tykes,
Help him, O Lord.
Raker of leaves, cleaner of eaves,
Dryer of dishes, fulfiller of wishes. . . .
Bless him, O Lord.

Jo Ann Heidbreder

Acknowledgments

The editor and the publisher have made every effort to trace the ownership of all copyrighted material and to secure permission from copyright holders of such material. In the event of any question arising as to the use of any material the publisher and editor, while expressing regret for inadvertent error, will be pleased to make the necessary corrections in future printings. Thanks are due to the following authors, publishers, publications and agents for permission to use the material indicated.

AMERICAN GIRL, a magazine published by Girl Scouts of the U.S.A., for "My Father" by Dawn Belt and "Dad" by Connie Vanco reprinted from the June 1973 issue.

RICHARD ARMOUR, for "Transportation Problem" by Richard Armour from *What Cheer* edited by David McCord.

CHRISTIANITY TODAY, for an excerpt ("What is a Father?") from "A Message to Fathers" by Edith Schaeffer reprinted from the April 26, 1974 issue. Copyright © 1974 by *Christianity Today*.

JOHN CIARDI, for "One Morning" from *Person to Person* by John Ciardi. Copyright © 1964 by Rutgers, The University Press.

HARPER & ROW, PUBLISHERS, INC., for an excerpt from *How to be a Father* by Frank B. Gilbreth, Jr. (T. Y. Crowell). Copyright © 1958 by Frank B. Gilbreth, Jr. and James J. Spanfeller.

HARPER'S BAZAAR, for an excerpt from "What Makes A Good Father," by Dr. Sol Gordon reprinted from the July 1975 issue. Copyright © 1975 by The Hearst Corporation.

HIGHLIGHTS FOR CHILDREN, INC., Columbus, Ohio, for "Walking" by Grace Ellen Glaubitz. Copyright © *Children's Activities*.

HOLT, RINEHART AND WINSTON, for excerpt ("Father Knew All The Answers") from *Over the Fence Is Out* by Jonathan Rhoades. Copyright © 1961 by Holt, Rinehart & Winston.

KING FEATURES SYNDICATE, INC., for excerpt from *Treasury of Reader's Digest Wit & Humor* by Louis Sobel. Copyright © 1946 by King Features Syndicate, Inc.

J. B. LIPPINCOTT COMPANY, for "Crayons" from *Poems* by Christopher Morley. Copyright © 1929, © renewed by Christopher Morley.

LITTLE, BROWN AND COMPANY, for "Some of My Best Friends Are Children" by Ogden Nash. Copyright © 1933, 1936, 1945, 1946, 1950, 1959 by Ogden Nash. British Commonwealth rights granted by Curtis Brown, Ltd.

Photo Credits

Designed by Daryl D. Johnson
Selected by Barbara Shook Hazen
Set in Benguiat Book and Helvetica